FOCUS ON CURRENT EVENTS

IMMIGRATION

by Patricia Sutton

www.focusreaders.com

Copyright © 2024 by Focus Readers®, Lake Elmo, MN 55042. All rights reserved. No part of this book may be reproduced or utilized in any form or by any means without written permission from the publisher.

Focus Readers is distributed by North Star Editions:
sales@northstareditions.com | 888-417-0195

Produced for Focus Readers by Red Line Editorial.

Content Consultant: Frank Argote-Freyre, PhD, Professor of History, Kean University

Photographs ©: Shutterstock Images, cover, 1, 4–5, 6, 9, 15, 17, 18–19, 21, 26, 30–31, 32, 36–37, 39, 41, 42–43; iStockphoto, 10–11; Photo Researchers/Science History Images/Alamy, 13; Eric Gay/AP Images, 22; Travis Long/The News & Observer/TNS/Newscom, 24–25; Red Line Editorial, 29, 45; David Goldman/AP Images, 35

Library of Congress Cataloging-in-Publication Data
Names: Sutton, Patricia, author.
Title: Immigration / by Patricia Sutton.
Description: Lake Elmo, MN : Focus Readers, 2024. | Series: Focus on
  current events | Includes index. | Audience: Grades 4-6
Identifiers: LCCN 2023005635 (print) | LCCN 2023005636 (ebook) | ISBN
  9781637396414 (hardcover) | ISBN 9781637396988 (paperback) | ISBN
  9781637398050 (pdf) | ISBN 9781637397558 (ebook)
Subjects: LCSH: United States--Emigration and immigration--Juvenile
  literature.
Classification: LCC JV6465 .S88 2024 (print) | LCC JV6465 (ebook) | DDC
  325.73--dc23/eng/20220227
LC record available at https://lccn.loc.gov/2023005635
LC ebook record available at https://lccn.loc.gov/2023005636

Printed in the United States of America
Mankato, MN
082023

ABOUT THE AUTHOR

Patricia Sutton is a writer and former elementary school teacher based in Madison, Wisconsin. She has an MFA in Writing for Children and Young Adults from Hamline University and is the author of two other books. She especially enjoys researching and writing narrative nonfiction for kids.

TABLE OF CONTENTS

CHAPTER 1
Why People Migrate 5

CHAPTER 2
A Brief History of US Immigration 11

CASE STUDY
US Actions and Immigration 16

CHAPTER 3
Refugees and Asylum Seekers 19

CHAPTER 4
Visas and Documentation 25

CHAPTER 5
Detention and Deportation 31

CHAPTER 6
Pathways to Citizenship 37

CASE STUDY
DACA 40

CHAPTER 7
Common Misconceptions 43

Focus on Immigration • 46
Glossary • 47
To Learn More • 48
Index • 48

CHAPTER 1

WHY PEOPLE MIGRATE

Sofiia had a decision to make. She and her children lived in Ukraine. But in February 2022, Russian troops invaded her country. Relatives in the United States urged Sofiia to get out while she could. She didn't want to leave her home. But she also wanted to keep her kids safe. So, she and her children found a flight to Mexico.

In Mexico, a relative picked up Sofiia and her kids. He drove them north. They came within

Russian attacks on Ukraine in 2022 destroyed many homes and buildings, causing millions of people to flee the country.

▲ By 2023, Title 42 had been used to turn back more than 2.5 million immigrants from the US–Mexico border.

inches of US soil. But Customs and Border Protection (CBP) agents refused to let them into the country. CBP is an agency that checks travelers' documents and works to keep US borders secure. CBP agents stopped Sofiia because of an order called Title 42. This order had been made in 2020, during the COVID-19 pandemic. A virus was spreading quickly around the world. US officials said Title 42 would slow it down. Health experts strongly disagreed. But in 2022, Title 42 was still being used.

Sofiia's relative explained that Sofiia was trying to escape a war. He asked if he could bring her to seek **asylum** in the United States. But the CBP agents said no. So, the family drove back to Mexico.

The next day, Sofiia and her children tried again. This time they walked to the border. Sofiia showed her passport, and a guard waved her to the side to wait. But another CBP agent told her to go away. Sofiia huddled with her children and cried. She didn't know what to do.

A lawyer named Blaine Bookey saw Sofiia and decided to help. Bookey knew the US government could make an exception to Title 42. So, she texted people she knew at CBP. She also shared

Sofiia's story on social media. Several other lawyers also helped. Eventually, Sofiia was able to cross the border. She and her kids were free to seek asylum in the United States.

Immigrants are people who leave their country and move to a new one. There are many reasons why they go. Some people move because of problems such as wars, natural disasters, or fear of **persecution**. These problems are sometimes called push factors. Other people immigrate because a new country offers opportunities. These reasons are called pull factors. People may want better jobs or education. Or they may want to join family members living in another country.

However, immigrating is not as simple as crossing a border. Moving to a new country often involves lots of paperwork and waiting. It can be confusing. It can also cost lots of money.

▲ Some people camp near the US–Mexico border, hoping to seek asylum after crossing.

Additionally, life in a new country can be difficult. The country may have languages, foods, and customs that are unfamiliar. Immigrants often have trouble finding jobs, transportation, and housing. They can face prejudice in their new home. These challenges can seem overwhelming. But many people feel that immigrating is their only option. These problems and what to do about them are just some reasons why debates about immigration remain common.

CHAPTER 2

A BRIEF HISTORY OF US IMMIGRATION

Indigenous peoples have lived in North America for thousands of years. In the 1500s, Europeans began starting **colonies** in North America. These Europeans took land from native nations. They also brought diseases that were new to Indigenous people. Millions of Indigenous people died as a result.

By the 1600s, the English, Dutch, Spanish, and French all had colonies in North America.

From the 1500s to the 1700s, several European countries raced to start colonies in North America.

At first, the Europeans settled along the East Coast. But then they moved west. They took more land from Indigenous peoples. After the United States became independent in 1776, its leaders continued taking land.

Throughout the 1800s, many immigrants came to the United States from Europe, Asia, and Latin America. They fled unrest and poverty at home. They hoped to find new opportunities. Most of these immigrants settled in large cities. Many took low-paying jobs that no one else wanted.

Some Americans looked down on these new immigrants. They made laws limiting who could enter the country. The Chinese Exclusion Act passed in 1882. It banned Chinese workers from coming to the United States. But other immigrants kept coming. Between 1880 and 1920, more than 20 million people arrived from Europe.

▲ Thousands of Chinese immigrants came to the United States in the 1800s to find work building railroads.

Meanwhile, anti-immigrant feelings were growing. So, Congress passed the Immigration Act of 1924. It set strict quotas. These limits said only a certain number of people from certain countries could enter each year. Immigrants from Asian countries were not allowed at all.

During World War II (1939–1945), millions of people in Europe lost everything. Thousands of homes, towns, and farms were destroyed. People needed new places to live. Many wanted to move

13

to the United States. At first, the US government would not accept these **refugees**. Later, it did allow some of them in. But it still kept strict limits based on quotas.

The ban on immigrants from Asia ended in 1952. And in 1965, the Immigration and Nationality Act brought other changes. This act made it easier for people from non-European countries to enter the United States. It also allowed Americans to **sponsor** family members who wanted to immigrate. Even so, most countries received a limited number of visas per year.

In the 1980s, new laws made it easier for more people to move to the United States. But that

➤ THINK ABOUT IT

Why might a country not want to accept refugees?

▲ The Department of Homeland Security sends workers to patrol the border and keep people from crossing illegally.

changed on September 11, 2001. After foreign terrorists attacked US buildings, the policy shifted again. The government made stricter rules about who could enter the country. It also created the Department of Homeland Security. This group focused on enforcing laws and border security.

Even so, people continued moving to the United States. In 2022, nearly 25 percent of people living in the country were immigrants or the children of immigrants.

CASE STUDY

US ACTIONS AND IMMIGRATION

Some US leaders have tried to stay separate from international issues, such as accepting refugees. But many US actions have major impacts on other countries. Starting in the 1800s, the US government backed companies that did business in Latin America. These companies often pushed out local landowners. They also paid low wages. This led to a spike in poverty and violence in the region. Some workers revolted. Their countries' governments responded by clamping down. People were killed or had their rights taken away. Many fled to the United States.

Fighting by US troops around the world has also created many refugees. For example, the Vietnam War (1954–1975) displaced 13 million people. More than one million fled to the United

⚠ The United States fought a war in Afghanistan from 2001 to 2021. This conflict displaced more than six million people.

States during and after the war. Since 2001, conflicts involving US troops have displaced more than 38 million people.

Climate change impacts immigration, too. About 25 percent of all **CO_2 emissions** come from the United States. These emissions make severe weather more likely. Severe weather can destroy homes or cause areas to run out of food and water. As a result, people may be forced to move.

CHAPTER 3

REFUGEES AND ASYLUM SEEKERS

Many people around the world are unsafe in their home countries. A country may be at war. Or the government may be corrupt. So, people may choose to flee. Leaving home is difficult. People must often make long, dangerous journeys. But staying can be even riskier. Some people may be killed if they don't leave.

People who leave home because of danger often become refugees. The United Nations (UN)

In the 2010s, conflict in Syria and nearby countries caused many people to flee the area.

19

gives this status to people who it determines have reasons to fear persecution. The UN is a group of countries that work together to solve problems. Part of this work involves helping people who are persecuted or displaced.

Race and religion are common reasons for persecution. But it can be based on many things. Someone's political beliefs can also make them a target. So can their sexuality or gender.

People apply to become refugees while in their home countries. The UN provides paperwork so they can cross borders and move somewhere safe. However, not everyone who flees their home country qualifies for refugee status. These people may seek asylum instead.

The first step in seeking asylum is getting into the United States. Once on US soil, asylum seekers must identify themselves. They must pass

▲ Political turmoil and lack of jobs and money in Venezuela have caused more than seven million people to leave the country since 2015.

security checks. And they must have evidence that returning home would be too risky. For example, they may come from an area with gang violence. Or they may be fleeing damage from a natural disaster. Domestic violence and extreme poverty can be causes as well.

Asylum seekers present this evidence to an asylum officer. The officer interviews them and decides if the danger seems credible. If so, a court

▲ While their applications are being processed, asylum seekers may be held at detention centers.

date is set. On this date, a judge will give them official asylee status. However, people may have to wait a long time. Thousands of people apply for asylum each year. As of 2022, the average case took more than four years to be finalized.

Asylum seekers who are waiting for their court date do have some rights. They can apply for work permits after 150 days. They can attend school. And they can move freely around the United States. However, they cannot return to their home country. They can't even go back for family emergencies.

Once asylee status is issued at the court hearing, people can apply for **Social Security** cards. They can request to travel internationally. They can also ask to bring family members to the United States. After one year, asylees can be given permanent legal status. And after five years, they can apply for citizenship. However, this process often involves even more waiting.

THINK ABOUT IT ◁

How are refugees and asylum seekers alike? How are they different?

CHAPTER 4

VISAS AND DOCUMENTATION

Many people who want to enter the United States must apply for visas. A visa is an official document that allows a person to travel to a foreign country. It gives the government information about the person.

There are several different types of visas. Temporary visas let people visit the United States for a short period of time. Some visas are for tourism. Others let people work or attend school.

H-1B visas let US companies hire immigrants with certain types of education or skills, such as software engineering.

⚠ Border patrol agents may arrest people who cross the border illegally or overstay their visas.

Each visa has an expiration date. At that time, the person must return to their home country. Staying in the United States beyond this date is illegal.

To stay in the United States long term, people must apply for an immigrant visa. The US government can give more than 675,000 immigrant visas each year. Some of these visas require a sponsor. For example, family-based visas go to people with close relatives in the United

States. Other visas are employment based. People need certain types of jobs or education to get them. Once in the United States, immigrant visa holders may apply for permanent legal residence.

The majority of US immigrants arrive legally. However, some enter the country without visas or other documentation. This is allowed only when people are seeking asylum. Otherwise, it is against the law.

Even so, some people try to cross the border without being noticed. People may pay guides to bring them into the country. This process tends to be difficult and dangerous. Each year, hundreds of people die trying to cross the US border. But some people feel they have no other choice. They may face even worse conditions at home.

Less than 25 percent of immigrants in the United States are undocumented. About half of them entered the country illegally. The others came with visas but stayed after their documents expired. Sometimes, people without the correct documents get caught. If that happens, they can be deported. That means they are sent back to their home countries. To avoid this, people may hide their undocumented status.

Most jobs in the United States require visas and paperwork. So, undocumented immigrants may struggle to find work. They may take jobs that are dangerous. Fear of deportation can keep them from reporting unsafe conditions. Getting health care and housing can be hard as well.

Some Americans wonder why anyone would enter the country illegally. Many people think immigrants should simply apply for visas and wait their turn. However, the immigration process can be difficult and expensive. It's also harder for some people than others. If people don't have family or work sponsors, the process can take years. In addition, 67 countries do not have a US visa processing center. To move to the United States, people there would have to first move to a third country.

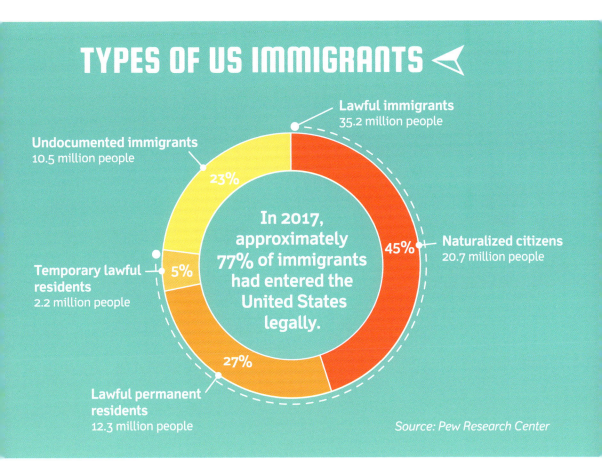

CHAPTER 5

DETENTION AND DEPORTATION

The United States accepts more immigrants than any other country in the world. More than one million arrived in 2022. Most came through legal means. They stood in lines at ports of entry. Ports of entry are places, such as airports, where people can enter a country. At each one, CBP agents inspect travelers' IDs. They also ask questions. If everything looks good, travelers can continue their journeys. However,

The United States has more than 300 of ports of entry.

▲ More than 100 checkpoints near US borders stop travelers to recheck their permission to enter.

some travelers are stopped. They must wait while agents investigate and decide if they can enter the country. This delay is called being detained.

For some people, detention lasts a few hours. Other people are held for several days. After interviews or investigation, some immigrants are released. They may be given a notice to appear in court. Or they may be free to go. Other immigrants are not released. Instead, they are sent to a residential facility. Many of these detention centers are run by Immigration and

Customs Enforcement (ICE). Like CBP, ICE is part of the Department of Homeland Security.

People may also be detained at checkpoints. These places are near US borders. Agents stop and check travelers who are moving from ports of entry to the rest of the United States. If people don't have the correct documentation, they can be sent to detention centers.

Supporters say detention protects the United States. They say it stops dangerous people from entering the country and keeps people from trying to avoid court or deportation.

However, detention has many critics. Travelers are often detained before it's determined if they can enter the country. So, innocent people may be detained. Plus, many detention centers were former jails. Detained people may be treated like criminals.

Detention facilities are supposed to provide food, places to sleep, and basic medical care. However, people have reported horrible conditions in many facilities. Buildings are often very cold. Detained people may sleep on concrete floors with thin blankets. Often, bright lights shine constantly. Many cells are very crowded. Some detained people don't speak English. They can't understand what guards are saying. Reports have also said sick people didn't get enough care.

The treatment of children raises particular concern. In 2018, the Department of Homeland Security announced a new, strict policy. It caused many undocumented families to be split apart at the border. Parents were **prosecuted** or deported. Children were sent to shelters. The shelters were made for unaccompanied minors, or children who entered the country alone. These kids could stay

▲ In late January 2023, approximately 24,000 immigrants were being detained in facilities across the country.

at the shelters until family or foster homes could care for them. However, the new law separated more than 5,000 children from their families. Some children remained in crowded shelters for months. Others never rejoined their families.

Critics suggest replacing detention with other options. Phone calls, apps, or ankle bracelets could track people's locations. However, these alternatives are also debated. They still treat the people like criminals, which most are not.

Application to Register Permanent Residence or Adjust Status

Department of Homeland Security
U.S. Citizenship and Immigration Services

SOCIAL SECURITY

UNITED STATES OF AMERICA

JUN 01 JAN 1990

Surname
DOE

Given N

ory:

geable:

artment of Homeland Security

e Center

CHAPTER 6

PATHWAYS TO CITIZENSHIP

Many immigrants want to become US citizens. The first step is getting a green card. This card gives an immigrant permanent residence. It allows the person to live and work in the United States. The person can get a driver's license and receive some government benefits, such as Social Security. People with green cards are free to travel to and from other countries as well.

A green card lasts for 10 years. After that, people must apply again.

People with immigrant visas receive green cards automatically after they arrive in the United States. Family members of a green card holder can apply for cards, too. So can people who marry US citizens. The application process often takes one to two years.

After green card holders have lived in the United States for several years, they can apply for citizenship. To do this, they fill out forms. They include documents to prove that their answers are correct. Next, applicants provide their fingerprints and go through security checks. An interview comes next. It proves they can speak, read,

➤ THINK ABOUT IT

If you were making laws about who could apply for citizenship, what requirements would you include? Why?

▲ At a naturalization ceremony, people pledge an oath and sign a certificate that makes them US citizens.

and write English. It also includes a civics test. This test asks questions about US history and government. People get two tries to pass.

Next, US government workers review each application. If approved, people attend a naturalization ceremony. During this event, they take an oath of allegiance to the United States. In this oath, people promise to follow US laws. They also pledge loyalty to the United States. After this ceremony, people are officially US citizens.

CASE STUDY

DACA

Some of the people who enter the United States without documentation are children. They may come on their own. Or their parents may bring them. Some of these children stay in the United States for years. If immigration officials find out about them, these young people can be deported. But some don't remember their home country. They may not even speak the language.

In 2012, President Barack Obama's **administration** created a program. It was called Deferred Action for Childhood Arrivals (DACA). The program provided a way for undocumented young people to stay legally. To apply, people had to have been under the age of 16 when they entered the country. They must have been in the United States the entire time since. They also needed to pass background checks. People who applied and qualified received a permit. It allowed

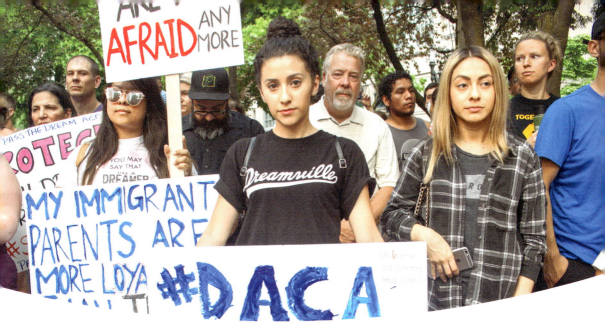

▲ Young people demonstrate in support of DACA.

them to work and attend school. Every two years, they could renew it. People could use this permit to get a driver's license and Social Security card, too.

Many Americans supported DACA. They felt it helped young people and the United States. Some even wanted to give undocumented young people a path to citizenship. However, President Donald Trump's administration tried to end DACA. The Supreme Court ruled that it couldn't. But as of 2022, legal challenges continued.

CHAPTER 7

COMMON MISCONCEPTIONS

The immigration process is complicated. Sometimes, people end up believing things that are not true. For example, some people are afraid immigrants are taking over the United States. But in 2022, immigrants made up 14 percent of the population. That was about the same percentage as 100 years earlier.

Other claims say dangerous people can sneak into the country as refugees or asylum

Immigrants celebrate becoming US citizens in 2005. That year, 12 percent of US residents were immigrants.

43

seekers. Actually, both processes use many careful security checks. People may also claim immigration increases crime. However, studies show that people born in the United States are more likely than immigrants to be arrested.

Another myth is that immigrants take jobs away from US citizens. Surveys have found that immigrants mainly take jobs other Americans don't want. In fact, by owning businesses and paying taxes, immigrants help the economy.

Sometimes, the media reinforces false ideas. Immigration stories and photos often feature Latino people. This can make people think most immigrants come from Central and South America. But nearly as many people move to the United States from Asian countries each year.

Words can shape people's thoughts, too. Some stories claim there's an "invasion" at the border.

Or they refer to undocumented immigrants as "illegals" or "aliens." Crossing a border without inspection is illegal. However, the people themselves are not. And they are not invading. Experts say it's important to use precise language when talking about immigration. This can help spread facts instead of fear.

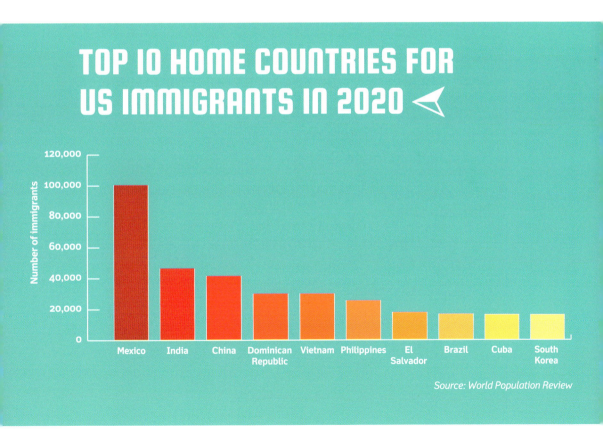

FOCUS ON
IMMIGRATION

Write your answers on a separate piece of paper.

1. Write a paragraph describing the main ideas of Chapter 6.

2. Would you support a plan to create a path to citizenship for undocumented immigrants? Why or why not?

3. Where do people who are fleeing to the United States from danger in their home country apply for asylum?

    A. in their home country
    B. from a third country
    C. in the United States

4. Which part of the immigration process do people go through first?

    A. getting an immigrant visa
    B. getting a green card
    C. becoming a US citizen

Answer key on page 48.

GLOSSARY

administration
The group of people who work in the government's executive branch under a specific president.

asylum
Protection given to people fleeing their country because of fear they will be harmed there.

climate change
A human-caused global crisis involving long-term changes in Earth's temperature and weather patterns.

CO_2 emissions
Gases that are released into the air, where they absorb and trap heat, causing climate change.

colonies
Areas taken over and controlled by a country that is far away.

persecution
Cruel and unfair treatment of people because of their beliefs or identity.

prosecuted
Brought to court, often as part of being charged with a crime.

refugees
People forced to leave their homes due to war or other dangers.

Social Security
A government program that gives money to people who are retired, disabled, or lacking income.

sponsor
To help another person apply to immigrate.

TO LEARN MORE

BOOKS

Kuklin, Susan. *We Are Here to Stay: Voices of Undocumented Young Adults*. Somerville, MA: Candlewick Press, 2019.

Smith-Llera, Danielle. *Immigration in America: Asylum, Borders, and Conflicts*. North Mankato, MN: Capstone Press, 2020.

Sutton, Patricia. *Asylum Seekers: Hope and Disappointment on the Border*. San Diego: ReferencePoint Press, 2023.

NOTE TO EDUCATORS

Visit **www.focusreaders.com** to find lesson plans, activities, links, and other resources related to this title.

INDEX

asylum, 7–8, 20–23, 27, 43

Chinese Exclusion Act, 12
citizenship, 23, 29, 37–39, 41, 44
Customs and Border Protection (CBP), 6–7, 31, 33

deportation, 28, 33–34, 40
detention, 32–35

green cards, 37–38

permanent residence, 23, 27, 29, 37

quotas, 13–14

refugees, 14, 16, 19–20, 23, 43

undocumented immigrants, 27–29, 34, 40–41, 45

visas, 14, 25–29, 38

Answer Key: **1.** Answers will vary; **2.** Answers will vary; **3.** C; **4.** A